Aerin Lauder
LIVING WITH FLOWERS

Aerin Lauder
LIVING WITH FLOWERS

Written with Jill Simpson

RIZZOLI NEW YORK

New York · Paris · London · Milan

For my mother, Jo Carole, who shared the joy of flowers with me
from a young age. From mini potted-geranium favors at my childhood birthday
parties to a bouquet waiting for me when I arrive home from a business trip,
she nurtured a lifelong love of nature, flowers, and all things beautiful.

Contents

Introduction

I can't imagine a world without flowers. When we take the time to observe them, both the immense variety and specificity of their beauty is extraordinary. Flowers touch so many senses: Their remarkable colors and shadings, intoxicating fragrance, fanciful shapes, and delicate, ornate textures all seem designed to delight us. They are simply beautiful for beauty's sake, without demanding anything in return beyond water and sunshine. What else gives so much joy for so little effort?

Nothing makes me happier than the gift of flowers from a friend's garden or a surprise delivery of peonies from my sons. Flowers are the way we express joy and celebration, congratulations and condolences, get-well wishes and treasured friendship. From enchanting first roses sent from an admirer to a bride's glorious bouquet to the blossoms set down to mark a loved one's passing, flowers mark each passage of life. But flowers aren't just for special occasions; you can surround yourself with them every day. Plants and flowers are nature's gift to us, and they needn't be elaborate or costly to offer delight. Some of the most appreciated gifts I've given are humble four-leaf clovers I've found and framed.

To me, flowers and photographs are what make a house a home—what make it personal and welcoming. Whether it's a bouquet of daffodils in the kitchen, a cheerful nosegay on my desk, or a lush centerpiece for a dinner party, flowers are an essential part of how I like to decorate and entertain. They are a worthy indulgence—I would say an essential. And while I treasure having fresh flowers, the artistry of flowers in porcelain or paintings, on wallpaper, fabric, and china gives me just as much joy.

In this book, I want to share with you the many ways I live with flowers and to inspire you to do the same. From a posy on my bedside table to greet me in the morning to flowering branches infusing my foyer with the scent of spring, flowers are my constant companion, a source of unmitigated joy in every season. I hope you will find the same.

A Legacy of Flowers

My earliest memory of my grandmother Estée was getting into the car with her and smelling the lush scent of Bulgarian rose—a perfume she had been developing. I also vividly remember the arrangements of scented flowers—often lilies or tuberose—that greeted guests in her entrance hall. Flowers are a portal to different people or places in my life: Scented geraniums remind me of my mother; calla lilies and tuberose of my grandmother. Lilacs remind me of East Hampton in summer, and orange blossoms instantly transport me to the Mediterranean. It's said that our sense of smell is strongly tied to memory because it is linked to the primal part of our brain where emotions and memories are formed. This is certainly the case for me. Flowers and fragrance are deeply intertwined in my memories of family and home.

I had a floral-wallpapered bedroom growing up, and my mother dressed my sister, Jane, and me in matching flowered dresses and nightgowns from Laura Ashley and D. Porthault. At my birthday parties, the favors for my friends weren't candy or toys, like all the other children's, they were small potted geraniums. Perhaps I've even passed this appreciation for flowers onto my sons, who always send me roses on my birthday (likely with some assistance from my mother). My mother sends me lilies of the valley to mark the start of spring. One of the most thoughtful gifts I've ever received was from my husband's aunt, who planted a cutting garden for me at our East Hampton home for my fiftieth birthday. Now, in addition to my hydrangea and lilac bushes, I have beautiful flowers to cut for arrangements all summer long.

My grandparents Estée and Joe, ready to greet guests in the foyer of their Palm Beach house. Estée always had a large bouquet of flowers, such as these lush mums, to welcome everyone into their home.

Flowers are not only an integral part of my family, but also of our family business. My grandmother Estée had an excellent nose for fragrance, and she developed so many best-selling Estée Lauder perfumes over the course of her career. One of her favorites, Beautiful, which she called her "garden of wildflowers," encapsulated the scent of "two thousand fresh flowers." She always took pleasure in surrounding herself with flowers, whether bouquets at the office and at home, glorious gardens at each of her homes, lavish centerpieces for dinner parties, or even whimsical beaded flowers at her home in Palm Beach. I remember once when we'd been having a hard time landing on just the right scent for our next AERIN fragrance, I walked past Estée's fragrant lilac bushes in East Hampton and realized we should change course and focus on this simple, transporting scent.

Flowers played a key role in Estée's elaborate marketing and entertaining events, from wildflowers flown in from the South of France for a fragrance launch to the entire La Scala opera house in Milan filled with 18,000 flowers tinted Estée Lauder blue in her honor. This legacy of a love of flowers from my mother and grandmother has grown into an incredible passion of mine today. Let me share it with you.

OPPOSITE, CLOCKWISE FROM TOP LEFT: Estée was always surrounded by flowers: At La Scala opera house in Milan, surrounded by thousands of flowers tinted Estée Lauder blue in her honor; in Palm Beach, with a bouquet of beaded flowers; with my sister, Jane, and me in a Norman Parkinson portrait; and at her desk mixing fragrances.

"My favorite flowers are whichever ones happen to be in season, and I take great pleasure in doing the flowers myself when we entertain at home."

—*Estée Lauder*

Estée relished entertaining in her Palm Beach dining room, with its hand-painted Gracie floral wallpaper and her table set with opulent crystal candelabra, gilded cut-crystal goblets, and, as always, fresh flowers.

Capturing the
Essence of Flowers

Flowers are remarkable because not only do we experience their beauty visually but also through our sense of smell. The fragrances that we've developed for AERIN reflect my love of flowers and have floral notes at their essence. They may be blended with other woody or spicy notes, but always there are flowers. Developing a fragrance is like cooking or composing music—balancing the different notes and chords to create something unique, distinctive, and captivating. I work with many talented perfumers, like Honorine Blanc, who help me capture the scent, mood, sense of place, and feeling that I have in mind. "For example, when we wanted to create a scent that evokes the Mediterranean, we blended honeysuckle with citrus notes from bergamot and mandarin, something that sparkles when you smell the fragrance and helps you to escape to this place," says Honorine. Drawing from a palette of as many as three hundred different ingredients, she says, "we play with floral scents almost like you arrange a bouquet."

Today, I am following in my grandmother's footsteps. Light, feminine fragrances centered on florals that evoke many of the memorable places I've traveled to are a cornerstone of the AERIN brand, and I take an active role in creating them with the help of our expert perfumers.

The Simple Elegance
of White

If there's a color of flower I naturally gravitate toward, it is white. A monochromatic bouquet showcases the rich textures of each flower: the nearly infinite, tissue-thin layers of peonies to the tiny bells of lily of the valley; the sunny-yellow pincushion centers of daisies to the halo of stamens inside anemones. White flowers are effortless—you can mix and match freely, knowing that your arrangement will never clash and will complement, rather than compete with, your decor. And of course, there is no such thing as pure white. There is a vast range of whites that are tinged with yellow or green, creamy ivory, or the palest alabaster pink. Mixing textures and keeping some of the leaves and greenery in an arrangement gives white blossoms contrast and depth.

I have an all-white cutting garden in East Hampton that is filled with peonies, dahlias, delphinium, roses, and more. I love to cover my summer tables with these blooms, and I often use white flowers all throughout the house. I also love white florals in a fragrance—their scents tend to be clean and fresh. White is historically associated with innocence and purity, which is why it was traditionally used for bridal bouquets, but I simply find white to be modern, fresh, and sophisticated in an understated, rather than attention-grabbing, way. I carried a simple bouquet of lilies of the valley at my wedding and wore fragrant white gardenias in my hair. When you're not sure what to choose, white is a classic, always-right answer. For me, however, choosing white isn't a choice borne out of indecision, but one that is happy and intentional.

OPPOSITE AND FOLLOWING PAGES: I love the sophisticated simplicity of all-white flowers with touches of greenery in our Palm Beach living room. In a serene, monochromatic room, flowers have more impact, as with this arrangement of David Austin roses, hellebores, mini-allium, and tweedia in a vintage Italian ceramic urn. My Carolina Herrera dress matches the palette.

"My grandmother Estée introduced me to calla lilies; they were her favorite flower. She carried a bouquet of them on her wedding day in January 1930."

—*Aerin Lauder*

Calla lilies, here in a vintage Murano cut-glass vase on my mantel, always remind me of my grandmother. Place flowers in front of a mirror to amplify their impact in a lovely way.

ABOVE AND FOLLOWING PAGES: Flowers and greenery are woven throughout our Palm Beach living room, from a pair of Calamondin orange trees in Italian ceramic urns to a small bouquet of roses in a gold repoussé vase on the Louis XV desk. OPPOSITE: A skirted octagonal table with a dramatic arrangement of budding dogwood branches in an antique Chinese urn creates a gracious entrance into the room.

A Timeless Pairing

Blue and white—whether in the centuries-old Chinese porcelain vases my grandmother Estée collected (and the color inspiration for her beauty brand) or the Americana sponge-ware my mother favors—is a classic, always-appealing combination that marries effortlessly with flowers. I was fortunate to inherit my grandmother's collection of Chinese urns, which she displayed on brackets on the living room wall of what's now our East Hampton house. The scenic indigo landscapes are a crisp complement to leafy greenery or white flowers as well as bright pinks, oranges, and yellows. Blue and white works well with almost anything, and I find myself turning to this perennial pairing frequently.

OPPOSITE AND FOLLOWING PAGES: A pair of eighteenth-century Delft earthenware baluster vases, which belonged to legendary interior designer Alberto Pinto, filled with sprays of spirea create symmetry on the mantel. They are similar to my grandmother Estée's collection of Chinese porcelains in her East Hampton home, which I inherited, including this urn on the dining room buffet. An all-white centerpiece is filled with beautiful textures from a variety of flowers including sweet peas, clematis, veronica, fritillaria, scabiosa, allium, and lilac.
PAGES 32 AND 33: Smaller, single-flower bouquets of anemones in a fluted gilt beaker and hyacinth in a silver repoussé vase add a fragrant touch to a side table and desk.

The Romance
of the Rose

I have always loved roses—their transportive scent is incorporated into nearly all my fragrances. My grandmother Estée particularly loved the scent of Bulgarian Rose. It is also known as Damask or Damascene Rose and is revered for its luxuriant scent. It is a keynote in Beautiful—the perfume she worked on for six years. Roses have a classic, timeless beauty that I never tire of. I follow their evolution from nascent, tight buds into lush, layered blossoms that gradually unfurl, eventually leaving a fragrant shower of petals—and I find the most captivating bouquets incorporate flowers in all stages of bloom. Roses mix effortlessly into arrangements and elevate other flowers, but they are always magnificent on their own—even as a single stem in a bud vase. I tend to prefer single-color arrangements of roses rather than mixing colors, and their effect can vary greatly from the simplicity of white to the femininity of pink to the richness of red.

Roses, particularly red ones, are said to represent romance and passion, but rose lore attributes different meanings to each color: Yellow represents friendship; white, innocence, purity, and reverence; pink, admiration, gratitude, and joy; and orange, fascination and desire. In any color, they are always enchanting and one of the most universally loved flowers.

White roses, cut short, in a Murano cut-glass vase are a timeless classic.

RIGHT AND FOLLOWING PAGES: Cutting roses in my all-white garden in East Hampton, which provides an abundance of flowers for arrangements. My floral Giambattista Valli dress echoes the surroundings. A lush arrangement of white roses, hydrangea, viburnum, tulips, lilies, lilac, *Astrantia*, sweet peas, loosestrife, and more melds a rich array of textures and tones.

"Flowers have been a large part of my life for as long as I can remember. Both of my grandmothers had beautiful flower gardens. The love and joy that they brought me has just continued into this profession. What I love the most about this career is the joy and pleasure it brings people. That's what makes me happy."

—*Michael Grim*
Floral designer, Bridgehampton Florist

OPPOSITE AND FOLLOWING PAGES: White flowers come in a wide range of shades and textures, giving them richness and depth—from humble daisies and zinnias to lavishly layered dahlias and roses.

The Joy of Color

Color brings us joy. It's been shown to lift our mood, and I think it's a large part of why we respond so instinctively to flowers. The artistry of color in a bouquet can take your breath away. I love to experiment with color in flower arrangements because it's temporary—there's no long-term commitment required. You can be bold, take risks, and have fun. Arrangements can incorporate colors you might shy away from in more permanent elements—bright pink, orange, purple, sunny yellow, or lime green. A bouquet might be just a small spark of color in a corner or an exuberant, color-filled centerpiece that brings the whole room to life.

Channel your inner artist and mix colors from a wide palette. Experiment with analogous colors (those next to each other on the color wheel)—such as blue and purple, or pink, orange, and yellow. Or try pairing complementary hues that sit across the color wheel and energize each other: for example, add a splash of orange to blue, or mix red with a touch of green. Or you can simply combine colors intuitively, responding to what pleases your eye. Our response to color is highly personal, so indulge in what you love most.

If you look at nature, every color lives together harmoniously—there are no "wrong" combinations, nothing looks out of place. Study the rich gradations of color even within a single flower, from stamen to petal to stem. Draw on nature for inspiration, and you're unlikely to go astray. Take texture into account as well: Just as a mix of hues adds beauty and depth to an arrangement, so too does a range of textures, from tight buds to frilly petals, spiky foliage to plump berries.

Consider the palette of the room the flowers will be in—for example, in a predominantly blue-and-white room, bright pink or orange will add a vibrant and appealing counterpoint. Flowers are the essential finishing touch in any space—just look at the photos in any interior design magazine. They're what bring a room—and our spirits—to life.

Wild Japanese sweet peas introduce a delightful splash of purple to brighten a neutral room. I've collected a wide range of embossed and engraved silver mint julep cups and vases like this one from Talmaris, a favorite tableware store in Paris.

"Flowers are my strongest obsession. They're nature's purest form of beauty, and I can't get enough of them. Even one flower is like therapy for my soul—it lifts my spirits and reminds me of the simple wonders in life. In summer, I press flowers into my notebooks; finding them in winter is pure poetry, a memory rush. Flowers are an infusion of life."

— *Giambattista Valli*
Fashion designer

"When it comes to my work, flowers are always on my mind," says Giambattista Valli.
"They guide my pencil and markers and when the graphite or ink hits the paper, they suggest the silhouette as well as the smell of this woman and the colors she's going to use."

PREVIOUS PAGES: A rich still life of gilded vases, urns, and candlesticks from antiques dealers and stores, including a vase from the Neue Galerie in the center, extends the warm glow of the bright mimosa flowers. ABOVE: I love how the beautiful boiserie paneling in our 1928 apartment incorporates floral and laurel-leaf motifs. OPPOSITE: Sprays of yellow mimosa, a harbinger of spring that blooms in late winter, bring a ray of sunshine to the mantel in my New York living room.

HUBERT DE GIVENCHY
Galerie

GUIDE D'EXPOSITION
Paris, 8-23 juin 2022

CHRISTIE'S

"Humbled by the splendor of flowers, I allow myself to be guided by their ephemeral grace. In each bouquet, I celebrate nature, my creativity simply an interpretation of its timeless beauty through the seasons."

—*Eric Chauvin*
Floral designer, event planner and owner,
Chauvin Paris

Eric Chauvin, one of my favorite florists in Paris, created this exuberant bouquet of pinks and purples, including peonies and roses that feel as though they were just picked from the garden.

Heirloom Florals

Part of our appreciation of fresh flowers no doubt lies in their impermanence, but I have just as much admiration for the artistry that captures the beauty of flowers in a more lasting way. From my grandmother's collections of floral china to my own finds in antiques stores, art galleries, and the Paris flea market, flowers come to life for me in prints and paintings, china and glassware, fabrics and linens, and porcelain bouquets. Being surrounded by flowers in all forms brings me great joy. I recently purchased a pair of beautiful vintage books titled *Old Garden Roses* from the auction of noted collector Jayne Wrightsman. Printed in England in the mid-1950s, these oversize volumes contain exquisite plates of paintings by Charles Raymond. I rely on my library of books, art, and images to inspire everything from products and marketing campaigns to floral arrangements and interior design. I am in awe of an artist's ability to interpret the splendor of flowers, and I always enjoy the hunt for new treasures to add to my collections.

The elegant engravings of watercolors by Charles Raymond make this pair of books, *Old Garden Roses*, purchased at the Jayne Wrightsman auction, a treasured find.

A vibrant bouquet of mimosa, Icelandic poppies, roses, and ranunculus in analogous shades of yellow, orange, and red bring warmth and cheer to my dining room for a birthday luncheon.

"I believe that when someone received flowers, those flowers represent the feelings of the sender, which is quite a powerful expression to translate."

—*Zezé*
New York City florist

OPPOSITE AND FOLLOWING PAGES: Zezé is a beloved New York City floral designer who I can always rely on to create colorful, optimistic, and joyful arrangements. For a birthday luncheon for a close friend, I ordered these charming pastel petit fours with tiny flowers from Bon Vivant. Icelandic poppies have such exquisite, artistic coloration in their delicately ruffled petals that a vase of just two or three can be all you need.

"Being able to fill the house with flowers from the garden brings me more joy than words can say. I love the frothiness of it all: the creaminess of the rambling roses, the wow of the peonies, the heavenly scent from the Philadelphus, and the daintiness of the sweet peas dancing around amongst it all."

—Willow Crossley
British floral designer

When we're hosting events in London, I often rely on the wonderful floral designer Willow Crossley, who's based in the Cotswolds. Her work has a very natural, abundant feel to it, as is evident in this arrangement of peonies and garden roses.

ABOVE, OPPOSITE, AND FOLLOWING PAGES: Shades of lavender and purple, set against complementary green foliage, have a soft, enticing beauty that's not as sweetly feminine as pink.
Stems of Japanese sweet peas branch out naturally from a silver vase, while anemones, with
their striking dark centers and delicate petals, are clustered in tighter arrangements in
mint julep cups. I think the combination of silver and lavender is an especially pretty one.

The Language of Flowers

During the Victorian era strict rules of etiquette constrained courting couples from speaking freely about their emotions, so they often communicated through flowers. Learning the symbolism of flowers was all the rage in the 1800s, particularly after the 1819 publication of *Le Langage des Fleurs* by Charlotte de la Tour in France, one of the earliest books on the subject. Literary, mythological and folkloric associations were assigned to each flower, according to its color and characteristics. Red tulips, for example, meant a declaration of love, while bluebells expressed kindness. But flowers could have negative connotations as well: A yellow carnation sent back to a would-be suitor could signal disdain, while sending ivy meant only friendship was desired. Over time, many of the meanings have changed or been forgotten, but I think it's fun to consider the secret language of flowers when sending them as a gift. A dear friend sent me lilies of the valley with a note about their association with happiness, which I found so thoughtful. If you, too, would like to start speaking "the language of flowers," here is a glossary to get you started.

Amaryllis—pride, success, and creativity

Anemone—short-lived, these represent fragility

Aster—daintiness and charm; affection

Baby's breath—everlasting love

Bells of Ireland—good luck

Bird-of-paradise—freedom

Bluebells—kindness

Calla lily—beauty or rebirth and resurrection

Camellia: pink—I miss you; white—purity, innocence, or admiration and respect

Chrysanthemum—honesty, friendship

Cornflower or bachelor's button—a good luck charm linked to wealth and good fortune

Cosmos—order and harmony

Daffodil—new beginnings, friendship, forgiveness

Dahlia—dignity, or change

Daisy—innocence and loyalty

Delphinium: open-hearted, youth, and renewal

Freesia—friendship, innocence, and trust

Gardenia—secret love or simply to say "you're lovely"

Geranium—true friendship

Gladiolus—integrity and strength, faithfulness and sincerity, generosity

Heather—good luck

Hibiscus—beauty

Holly—domestic happiness

Hollyhock—ambition

Hyacinth: purple—"Please forgive me"

Hydrangea—"Thank you for understanding"

Iris—royalty, wisdom, respect, or "I have a message for you"; blue—faith and hope

Ivy—friendship

Jasmine: white—sweet love, beauty, appreciation

Lavender—devotion

Lilac—love and passion

Lily: white—sympathy, but also purity and rebirth; pink—prosperity; orange—pride; yellow—gratitude

Lily of the valley—purity, return of happiness, luck, humility

Magnolia—love of nature

Marigold—passion and creativity

Mimosa—secret love

Morning glory—affection

Myrtle—good luck and love in marriage

Narcissus—"Stay as sweet as you are"

Olive branch—peace

Orchid—love, beauty, refinement, wisdom

Pansy—thoughtfulness and remembrance

Peony—bashfulness, or romance and a happy marriage

Poppy: red—remembrance

Ranunculus—radiant with charm

Rhododendron—danger

Rose: pink—grace, happiness, and gentleness; white—new beginnings, purity, and innocence; red—passion and romance

Rosemary—remembrance

Salvia: blue—thinking of you

Snapdragon—deception, or grace, strength, protection from evil

Stephanotis—marital bliss

Stock—lasting beauty, bonds of affection, a happy life

Sunflower—spirituality, good luck, and ambition

Sweet pea—blissful pleasure or goodbye

Tulip: yellow—sunshine; pink—caring, well wishes, happiness; red—declaration of love

Violet—loyalty, devotion, faithfulness, modesty

Zinnia—thinking of absent friends

Indoor Gardens

One very special way to live surrounded by flowers year-round is through the artistry of floral wallpapers and fabrics. My grandmother Estée had a beautiful hand-painted Gracie wallpaper in her iconic office in New York City and in her dining room in Palm Beach that captivated me as a young girl, and I later used that same paper in my dressing room in our New York apartment. Transportive, romantic, feminine, the wallpaper's intricately detailed flowering trees, where birds and butterflies alighted, made me feel like I had escaped to an enchanted oasis within the city. But floral and scenic wallpapers are not only for personal or feminine spaces. They can be equally compelling in a dining room, setting guests amidst an elegant Eden; in an entry foyer, gracefully bridging indoors and out and creating a dramatic first impression; or in a powder room or bath, where their delicacy and detail can transform a utilitarian space into a jewel box.

In our Palm Beach house, built in 1930, I knew I wanted to create such a fantasy moment in the dining room to reflect not only my love of nature but the lush tropical gardens surrounding the house. I had long admired a hand-painted floral fabric in my friend Deeda Blair's Manhattan bedroom. She generously allowed us to borrow one of the curtain panels, and designer Stephen Sills had artists Jay Lohmann and Podge Bune artfully recreate its climbing roses, full-blown tulips, and leafy vines against a light, airy ground. It blends whimsy with sophistication and immediately sets the scene of an alluring indoor garden.

OPPOSITE AND FOLLOWING PAGES: Artists Jay C. Lohmann and Podge Bune transformed our Palm Beach dining room into an enchanting garden with exquisite hand-painted flowers on silk. The lavender oversize check tablecloth from Cowtan & Tout provides a crisp yet soft counterpoint. An arrangement of white roses and peonies paired with delicate lily of the valley in silver cups complements, rather than competes with, the walls. A dress from Victoria Beckham in a fresh spring green feels right in this floral fantasy of a room.

If Walls Could Talk

Our new Manhattan apartment is in a wonderful classical building designed by Rosario Candela and Warren and Wetmore in the late 1920s. The apartment has many elegant architectural details that I did not want to alter, including a remarkable antique wallpaper that I immediately fell in love with. The wallpaper panels date from the 1700s and had been installed in the dining room many decades ago. What makes the wallpaper particularly special are the pairs of birds, often looking at each other, which signify friendship and love. There are also two birds fighting over a worm—an unusual touch of humor and whimsy for that era. When we had the wallpaper restored, the restorer told me this bird-pair motif is quite rare. The design harmonizes flawlessly with the fireplace mantel and other architectural elements.

Scenic wallpapers like this tell a story and bring a rich narrative quality that perfectly suits a social setting like a dining room. The scenes portrayed can be a conversation starter or they can simply make people feel immersed in a captivating environment that brings any gathering to life.

The scenic wallpaper in our Upper East Side apartment dining room dates from the 1700s and features delicate leafy branches and birds against a pale-pink ground, setting a magical backdrop for dinners around the antique English Regency dining table.

This is a classic table—
crisp, light, and timeless—
I never tire of: silver,
crystal, white linens, and
an abundant, all-white
bouquet filled with garden
roses, tulips, sweet peas,
stock, and ranunculus,
and smaller satellite
arrangements of sweet
peas and hellebores in
silver cups and bud vases.

"Every petal I'm making, it's like I'm in my garden and I'm just feeling the flower; I'm not trying to make it a scientific study, it's just the joyful feeling of that flower. I'm striving to capture the soul of the flower."

— *Clare Potter*

Ceramic artist

Clare Potter's lifelike arrangements, such as this one of pink and purple anemones, are painstakingly crafted from high-fire ceramic clay and then painted in many layers of thin acrylic washes to create natural, luminous color. Her sculptures can take a month or more to create.

ABOVE: In our living room, a Louis XIII Savonnerie carpet, circa 1640, given to us by my father, features lush arrangements of flowers and fruits. I purchased the gilded Louis XVI bergère at the Givenchy auction. OPPOSITE: The remarkable eighteenth-century wallpaper panels in our Manhattan dining room feature lively birds hunting for worms or looking at each other. They were meticulously installed to fit naturally around the architectural elements in the room, including the ornate mantel.

Painted on Porcelain

My grandmother Estée collected floral china, which she loved to use when she entertained. I inherited much of it, and I like to mix and match the vintage and antique patterns to create a beautiful and feminine table. Floral-patterned china and porcelain enjoy an illustrious heritage. Marie-Antoinette, for example, always wanted to be surrounded by flowers at the Petit Trianon and had their likeness recreated on every surface— embroidered and woven into fabric, carved into wood, and sculpted and painted on porcelain. She commissioned elaborate china services from the royal manufacturers of Sèvres and Limoges. The Marie-Antoinette dinnerware pattern adorned with cornflowers and pearls is still manufactured to this day by Bernardaud.

Flora Danica, another historic floral porcelain with a remarkable heritage, has been made by Royal Copenhagen for over 230 years. It's based on a botanical encyclopedia commissioned by King Frederik V of Denmark in the 1750s that cataloged more than three thousand flowers growing in Denmark. The next king commissioned what he hoped would be the most impressive dinner service in the world, with more than 1,800 pieces of porcelain, each hand-painted with a different flower from the *Flora Danica* encyclopedia. This china collection has become one of Denmark's greatest cultural treasures. To this day, every piece of Flora Danica china is still hand-painted to order in the likeness of one of the thousands of flower illustrations. From Chelsea Porcelain, made since the 1700s in England, featuring botanical illustrations and butterflies, to the classic Botanic Garden pattern made by Portmeirion since the 1970s, flowers have never stopped being a beloved motif for fine china in almost every culture and through each century to the present day.

My grandmother Estée collected floral china such as these gilt- and scalloped-edge plates, which I inherited. I enjoy mixing and matching different patterns at a dinner party—I think it makes for a lively table.

I found this 1960s Chantilly porcelain dinner service at a Paris flea market.
It's hand-painted with a graceful blue carnation motif, or *l'œillet*, and
also features raised basketweave detail. The porcelain was made at the famed
Chantilly porcelain factory, north of Paris, which is no longer in existence.

"When my father served as US ambassador to Austria, my grandmother Estée, while visiting him in 1988, purchased a full set of Herend porcelain in its classic 1860s pattern, Fruits & Flowers. On my fiftieth birthday, my mother generously gifted this set to me. If I ever want to serve dinner or tea for thirty, I'm covered!"

—*Aerin Lauder*

This elegant Herend porcelain pattern, Fruits & Flowers, is more than 150 years old. The rose finials on the teapot, coffeepot, and sugar bowls make it delightfully feminine. A small bouquet of pale-pink anemones and roses in a silver mint julep cup adds the perfect accent.

PREVIOUS PAGES: My parents gave me the ornate Meissen candelabra, which echoes the birds in the wallpaper. ABOVE AND OPPOSITE: I ordered this exquisite cake for a bridal shower from Made in Heaven Cakes in New York. It features pastry chef Victoria Zagami's intricate, lifelike fondant flowers.

A Glorious Gift

It's no secret that flowers are always a welcome and beloved gift. They're a luxury we might not indulge in for ourselves, a delightful surprise, and a radiant messenger of thoughtfulness, love, caring, or concern. Whether it's a thank-you after a special dinner party, a pick-me-up for a colleague, or to celebrate a treasured friend's birthday, I love to send flowers in a special vase, often one from my own collection. Going beyond the basic glass florist's vase to gift something I know someone will love and use long after the flowers have faded adds a more personal touch. Flowers are among the most thoughtful ways to express condolences, gratitude, and to celebrate a holiday or anniversary. Even better, consider sending them for no reason at all—you will truly make a special someone's day. Different varieties of flowers are said to have different meanings (see page 70 for a guide), so choosing a flower that symbolizes whatever sentiment you wish to express can add another layer of care to your gift. Add a short note explaining what your chosen flowers represent so your recipient can appreciate their significance.

Vases are a timeless, always appreciated gift as well. Silver mint julep cups, which can be engraved with a monogram, name, or special date, are particularly meaningful to me. I gave each of my bridesmaids a julep cup engraved with our wedding date, and a dear friend gave me silver cups engraved with each of my sons' names and birthdates as treasured baby gifts that I display and use to this day. I find that mint julep cups are just the right size and shape for a petite arrangement of flowers on a bedside table, at a desk, on the bar, or as smaller bouquets on a dining table. You could place one at each person's place setting, down the center of the table, or array them around a larger arrangement. Of course, they're perfect for actually holding mint juleps, iced tea, and other drinks (the silver keeps drinks quite cold) or to use as a stylish pencil cup. You will easily find a multitude of uses for these simple, timeless vessels. I have collected many over the years, some fluted, sculpted, or embellished in various ways.

When each of my sons was born, a dear friend gave me a silver mint julep cup engraved with their name and birthdate. They're wonderful keepsakes that I keep out and use regularly as vases. Here, they're holding frilly lavender sweet peas.

Rustic Charm

In a rustic setting like the mountains, a farmhouse in the country, or my parents' antique barn in East Hampton, I like to choose flowers and plants that complement natural materials like raw wood and aged bricks. Though the backdrop is casual, I still want the flower arrangements to feel substantial, befitting the surrounding woodlands. Flowers in rich, deep hues like crimson reds and tones of green, as well as my favorite classic whites, hold their own against the rugged textures. Other materials—hand-painted ceramics, natural terra-cotta, and wicker and rattan baskets and vases—meld effortlessly with the wooden floors and beams. Even in this pastoral setting, I will still sometimes use a fine tablecloth and crystal as a surprising counterpoint. Other times, a bare wood table set with olive-green plates, green spongeware, and wood- or bamboo-handled silverware suit each other perfectly. Branches, berries, lots of greenery, and a rich mix of textures bring arrangements to life and connect with the wooded views outside the windows. Candles and a fire in the fireplace contribute a cozy, romantic glow. In winter, I add more evergreens, pine boughs, and berried branches to fill the air with woodsy fragrance and bring the outdoors inside, a reminder of the abundance of life outside all year long.

In an early American barn on my parents' property in East Hampton, I enjoy setting a formal dinner table with china, crystal, and a floor-length tablecloth as an unexpected counterpoint to the rustic wood walls and Austrian folk chairs. A flower arrangement showcasing a lot of greenery and texture suits this woodsy setting, as does my dress from Vilshenko that features intricate flowers and birds.

Large and small bouquets of white and green wildflowers, blossoms, and foliage with varied textures, such as ranunculus, veronica, hellebores, Queen Anne's lace, bouvardia, and milkweed echo the ever-green sprigs in the tablecloth and the rugged backdrop of the barn. FOLLOWING PAGES: Full-blown, deep-red peonies and butterfly ranunculus contrast with a lacy bouquet of dill and alchemilla in complementary colors on this rustic wood table set with spruce-green pierced-ceramic plates and wood-handled flatware.

"Geraniums, with their bright, optimistic simplicity, have always been a favorite of mine—from the potted geraniums my mother always has in the country to lesser-known varieties such as ruffled-leaf Martha Washington and lavender-hued Azure Rush. Scented geraniums have also inspired my fragrances, such as Wild Geranium."

—*Aerin Lauder*

Small clusters of vibrant red dahlias, anemones, and *Hypericum* berries brighten an Americana table set with olive-green spongeware and modern glassware. The tulip motif on a 1700s Pennsylvania earthenware jar echoes the flowers.

ABOVE, OPPOSITE, AND PREVIOUS PAGES: At an autumn dinner, opulent burgundy peonies in full bloom show off their many-layered petals in exuberant arrangements with red *Hypericum* berries overflowing from woven baskets and earthenware pitchers. A single magnificent bloom in a simple crystal bud vase has outsize impact. The flowers are echoed in hand-painted artisanal plates from Portugal in a collaboration between Casa Lopez and AERIN. Carved wood-handled flatware adds another layer of texture.

Nature's Palette

In an outdoor setting—whether backyard, porch, or patio—flowers are naturally at home. With seemingly a thousand shades of green in trees, hedges, grass, and gardens forming the backdrop, flowers take center stage. With the relaxed ease of dining and entertaining outdoors, I like the natural informality of wildflowers, blowsy garden-picked blossoms, and a paint palette of colors that stands out against the verdant background. I love to arrange a mix of vases either lined down the center of a long table or clustered together at the heart of a round table. Each small vase might have a single type or color of flower, or a mix of pretty hues and textures to fill the table and bring a touch of beauty to each guest. A sense of generosity and abundance is achievable even with small bouquets and matches the fullness of the season. I like to mix and match an array of clear glass or crystal vases or use summery natural materials like woven raffia sleeves around glass cylinders. This gives the effect of a garden party, which is one of the most appealing themes to conjure on a warm spring or summer day. A colorful or floral-patterned tablecloth, flower- or leaf-entwined china, floral embroidered napkins, wicker placemats, and bamboo flatware continue the natural motifs throughout the table settings. Setting a beautiful table and creating eye-catching flower arrangements feels almost effortless in summer, when so much natural beauty surrounds us and all the ingredients are right at hand.

When we're in the country, I love to wake up early and go out into the garden and cut fresh flowers—like these fulsome blue hydrangeas—and arrange them in the kitchen before everyone awakens.

PREVIOUS PAGES, ABOVE, AND OPPOSITE: Nothing is prettier or easier than setting a lovely table outdoors in summer. With the wealth of the garden, local farmstands, and even roadside wildflowers, I like to mix a wide range of soft colors in loose, natural bouquets. Zinnia, tweedia, cupcake cosmos, astilbe, hellebores, clematis, and butterfly ranunculus all come together easily in white ceramic and clear glass vases. They mirror the flowered tablecloth, Italian hand-painted Florentina plates, and embroidered Fiore napkins from AERIN.

Woven wicker trays make it simple to serve an inviting lunch, tea, or cocktails outside. Glass and wicker vases hold simple garden blooms on a small table set out on the lawn with a pretty flower-strewn tablecloth in Vita from Lisa Fine Textiles. Soane Britain Rattan Carousel Chairs brought out from the kitchen coordinate with the tablescape's natural textures.

"My favorite flower arrangements are always the ones from Ottoman or Persian miniatures—carnation, tulip, rose, and hyacinth in long-necked bud vases. It allows you to create a landscape on your dinner table. For bigger arrangements, I like the informality of country flowers."

— *Carolina Irving*
Textile, tabletop, and home designer

OPPOSITE AND FOLLOWING PAGES: Hand-painted Portuguese ceramic plates in a mix of colors from Carolina Irving & Daughters for AERIN and Carolina's Mimosa Vine Tablecloth set a sunny, exuberant table outside. Layering with wicker place mats, bamboo flatware, and bouquets of colorful cosmos and dahlias nestled in woven-raffia vases makes for an enchanting midsummer afternoon or evening.

Sancia mouth-blown crystal vases from AERIN are smaller versions of traditional Chinese plum vases that were shaped specifically to hold a plum tree branch. A colorful mix of dahlias, cosmos, butterfly ranunculus, and clematis are arrayed down the length of the table so that everyone can enjoy their beauty. Hand-painted flourishes on bowls and plates evoke blossoms and leafy garlands.

At the Children's Table

When I was a little girl, creating fantasy tea parties for my stuffed animals and my devoted grandmothers, Estée and Sylvia, was one of my favorite pastimes and is probably why I love to entertain. Estée gave me a child's tea set that I still have today, and I still love the idea of designing fanciful settings for children. Of course, with two sons, those miniature tables were covered in dump trucks and dinosaurs, not tea sets, but that hasn't diminished my fantasy—maybe it's one I can create for granddaughters someday. I think children enjoy being treated to a special-occasion tea or lunch that's just for them. When some friends and their children came to visit, I indulged this vision with a child-size rattan table and chairs in a corner of the backyard. A child's tea set, some irresistible candies and fruits, and small-scale bouquets like lilies of the valley and pale-pink anemones in silver mint julep cups made the children feel like guests of honor. I find that children often rise to the occasion—if they're treated to fine things, they learn to take more care with them. And in a child-size setting—no adults allowed—they can indulge in flights of fancy and their own visions of sugarplums and snapdragons.

A charming children's tea party is set up in the garden on a miniature rattan table and chairs with a child's tea set and small-scale bouquets of blush-pink anemones and delicate lily of the valley in silver julep cups. Ceramic flowers mingle with bowls of enticing candies and sugar fruits.

At Home in the Kitchen

Please don't reserve flowers only for company or the more formal rooms in your home. If there is any place you will see and enjoy flowers most, in fact, it is probably your kitchen. The kitchen is where the whole family gathers, and where we often eat weekday meals, from breakfast at the island to family suppers. I might have a cluster of large palm fronds on the island to bring a dramatic dose of fresh greenery or a bunch of sunny daffodils in my whimsical Jeff Koons Puppy vase or topiaries flanking a kitchen window by the breakfast table. All bring color, nature, and cheer to this much-used area of the home. It doesn't take much to brighten a white kitchen—a bouquet of hydrangeas cut from the garden, a dozen tulips picked up from the greengrocer's, or branches of chrysanthemum pruned from a hedge in spring. When I'm serving more casual meals at the farmhouse table in our kitchen or in the breakfast room, I like to use smaller, more informal arrangements on the table—a medley of clear-glass bud vases with garden blossoms or greenery, or small potted plants. Sometimes I will set up a buffet on the island where guests can help themselves. Colorful bowls of fruit and pitchers of flowers make the display all the more inviting.

Even in my pantry, a grid of a dozen antique botanical engravings in whimsical découpaged frames brings the beauty of the garden to this practical room. I found this set of charming engravings at an antiques show in San Francisco some years ago, and I wasn't even sure where I would put them when I purchased them. Finally, when we bought this house in Palm Beach, I found the ideal spot for them. They provide a focal point and bring colorful artistry to this everyday space.

I like to set up informal buffets on my kitchen island—here with a stack of modern marbleized plates from Christopher Spitzmiller, colorful Murano glasses, floral-sketched napkins from Willow Crossley, and informal masses of bright flowers. My beloved Jeff Koons Puppy vase holds vibrant daffodils, while a simple white cachepot offers up an abundance of green parrot tulips in bud. In the background, a statuesque vase by Frances Palmer is the ideal vessel for large flowering branches of quince.

I love to arrange flowers I've cut from the garden and place them in containers throughout the house. Woven wicker and raffia vases and cachepots with glass liners are a natural home for branches of viburnum and hydrangea, stems of lilac, *Astrantia*, veronica, and spirea. Focusing my color palette makes arranging simple and sophisticated.

At our kitchen table in East Hampton, blue and white—in both flowers and tableware—form such a charming, inviting palette. Simple bouquets of blue *Muscari* (grape hyacinth) and white dahlias, anemones, and Queen Anne's lace effortlessly complement the blue spongeware plates on woven-straw place mats.

133

A tall glass cylinder vase is something every home should have. Here it holds large palm fronds and monstera leaves for a simple but dramatic arrangement in the kitchen of our Palm Beach home.

"We live in our kitchen—breakfast, lunch, and dinner. In fact, some of our best dinner parties have been around the kitchen table with friends and family. You know you're a close friend if you're invited for a casual dinner in the kitchen."

—*Aerin Lauder*

A favorite kitchen place setting: lacy, pierced Paulette plates from AERIN in a soft blue-green with a crisp, white monogrammed napkin and lots of natural texture from woven-wicker place mats and bamboo flatware, swirled Murano glassware, and, always, flowers.

Leafy branches have an appealing informality about them that adds shape to an arrangement. A central bouquet surrounded by a ring of small satellite vases includes privet, mayweed, hellebores, ranunculus, alchemilla, and bouvardia. The round table in our breakfast room is dressed in a Colefax & Fowler tablecloth, itself a garden of chrysanthemums and butterflies. FOLLOWING PAGES: In the pantry, a grid of a dozen botanical copper engravings done by Georg Dionysius Ehret in Germany in the 1700s are enhanced by whimsically découpaged frames, creating a captivating focal point for this otherwise utilitarian space.

Just for You

While many of us splurge on flowers only for entertaining and special occasions, I think the flowers you enjoy most are the ones you choose solely for yourself. A fragrant nosegay to wake up to each morning by your bedside, a lissome orchid brightening your bath, or a bud vase with a single perfect peony on your desk can bring beauty and delight to your everyday. If you invest in an orchid or flowering plant, you'll enjoy its company for many weeks to come, but just snipping a few hydrangeas from your yard or picking up a simple bunch of tulips at the market brings nature by your side, where you can enjoy it all day long.

A small, delicate bouquet—lilies of the valley, freesia, roses—fits easily on a bedside table. I also always keep flowers or plants, often orchids, in my bath, where they thrive on the humidity and make a personal space feel that much more pampering.

Beside my bed, to enjoy both their fragrance and beauty as I drift off to sleep and when I wake up: a bouquet of my favorite lilies of the valley in a small silver cup. The water glass hand-painted with the same flowers was a gift from a close friend. And you might not even realize the potted white dahlia is made of porcelain, a treasured work of art by Vladimir Kanevsky. I love all-white flowers in the bedroom next to elegant white lace-trimmed D. Porthault linens.

"In this guest room in Palm Beach, I was inspired by my grandmother to decorate the room en suite—wallpaper, fabrics, even lampshades—in a classic Bennison pattern, enveloping the room in a garden of delicate blossoms."

—*Aerin Lauder*

OPPOSITE AND FOLLOWING PAGES: The guest room becomes an enchanted bower wrapped floor-to-ceiling in Bennison's Chinese Paper, a delicate flower-strewn fabric and wallpaper. It's nicely balanced by the natural textures of sisal matting and a rattan bedside table. I always put fresh flowers, like these white hyacinths and roses, in guest rooms as a welcoming touch.

Forever Flowers

European artisans began crafting delicate blossoms in porcelain after discovering how to make soft-paste porcelain in the mid-1700s, in manufactories such as Vicennes in France, Meissen in Germany, and Chelsea in England. This venerable tradition has re-emerged with a more modern approach through artists working today, like Vladimir Kanevsky and Clare Potter, both of whose work I admire and collect. A special collection of Vladimir's pieces will be on display when the Frick Collection reopens in New York City in late 2024.

After training as an architect in the Soviet Union, Vladimir Kanevsky immigrated to the United States over thirty-five years ago. Also a talented sculptor, he moved here with very little money and had to find a way to pay his rent. He answered an ad he saw in an art supply store for a ceramicist, and then taught himself how to sculpt and fire porcelain, a notoriously fickle and challenging medium. The ad was from Howard Slatkin, an interior designer with a home-furnishings and antiques shop in New York. Vladimir's first assignment was to sculpt a melon, which took him a month and a half through trial and error. From fruits, he graduated to flowers and found his unexpected calling. His work is prized by many noteworthy designers and collectors such as Charlotte Moss, Carolyne Roehm, and Deeda Blair. "In the eighteenth century, porcelain flowers were extremely popular," says Kanevsky. "And it's interesting to keep up this tradition, but also make something completely different."

Artist Clare Potter is also known for her intricate floral sculptures, which she crafts from high-fire ceramic clay. She doesn't glaze them but instead painstakingly paints them with many layers of thin acrylic washes to get the exact colors she wants. "They're very soft looking because they're not glazed," says Potter. "And I think that's what makes them unique."

Vladimir Kanevsky's delicate porcelain flower sculptures are remarkably lifelike, especially in flowerpots, where they seem to grow naturally, but they are also exquisite works of art.

ABOVE: Laure de Chocqueuse, a French artist who painted the lilies of the valley on the tumbler by my bed, also hand-painted this treasured set of glasses. She lives in Normandy, France, and paints the flowers growing in her garden. OPPOSITE: Breakfast in bed is the ultimate luxury—something my grandmother Estée enjoyed, but I rarely have time for. To truly indulge a guest, use china, silver, and a linen napkin and add a petite vase of flowers as the perfect finishing touch.

Secret Gardens

Almost everywhere I've lived, I always try to carve out space for a dressing room. It is my private getaway where I can escape from the energy of two sons and my husband when I need to have a quiet moment to myself or get ready for the day or an evening out. In Palm Beach, I chose to envelop the room in a serene strié sky-blue glaze on the paneled walls and closets, then layered in florals through fabric and framed art. Vintage illustrations of pansies and carnations are framed in natural bamboo, and the cerulean Louis XV chair is upholstered in a classic Bennison flower-strewn linen. Even the ornate crystal Baguès chandelier with its feathery blue arms reminds me of delphinium.

For the dressing room in my New York apartment, working with designer Stephen Sills, we created a sophisticated, more unusual floral fantasy with the palest peach-pink silk-papered walls on which soft gray, black, and white flowers were hand-painted. The monochromatic climbing vines are an unexpected counterpoint to the shell-pink walls and curtains. These exquisite hand-painted florals make me feel like I've been transported to an enchanted garden. This is my inner sanctum, the place where I can indulge my most feminine side.

Don't shy away from surrounding yourself with flowers in personal spaces—done tastefully, motifs borrowed from nature are timeless and you will never tire of them. I find this space incredibly rejuvenating—it's where I begin and end my day, take time to read or talk on the phone with a friend, or take a short rest to recharge before a big event. If you don't have a dressing room, a comfortable chaise longue or armchair in your bedroom, a deep window seat, or a comfortable sofa in a sunroom or library can all serve as your private getaway. Bring in soft floral-chintz pillows, a side table to set down a cup of tea and small bouquet or plant, and you've created a sanctuary.

OPPOSITE AND FOLLOWING PAGES: The soft-blue strié-glazed walls and closets of my dressing room are beautifully calming. The AERIN shagreen dressing table is a luxurious spot to do my makeup and get ready for an evening out. A pair of late eighteenth-century English watercolors of pansies and carnations tie into the floral Bennison fabric on the chair. The pièce de résistance is the 1930s Maison Baguès French chandelier with blue-crystal arms that remind me of delphiniums.

"I grew up in a small North Carolina town surrounded by flowers, gardens, and small farms. I learned early on in my work not to focus on competing with nature, but to observe, interpret, and edit. I was, and continue to be, blessed to spend a lifetime doing what I love, and being surrounded by flowers."

—*Tommy Mitchell*
Toleware artist

Artist Tommy Mitchell began his career restoring art, statuary, and European toleware. From reconstructing leaves and blooms, he started creating his own beautiful floral sculptures from metal. His captivating artworks, including these morning glories and narcissus, are handcrafted from metal and painted, gilded, or done in natural zinc.

A Storied History

Hand-painted Chinese wallpapers date back to around 1750 and were originally created for export to Europe, according to Mike Gracie, of the esteemed family-run Gracie wallpaper company in New York City. These scenic wallpapers are believed to have evolved from Chinese scrolls and ink paintings, which included landscapes, flowers, and birds. In the late 1700s and early 1800s, when sea trade routes were established with China, the export market grew tremendously—first for tea, then for handcrafted products like porcelain and lacquerware. Originally, hand-painted wallpapers were produced in small batches as special gifts for important customers like sea captains or merchants, but the papers gradually grew in popularity. In the nineteenth century, the French started creating block-printed scenic wallpapers at firms like Zuber, which is the only one still in existence. In the early twentieth century, Charles Gracie's (Mike's grandfather) company became the first since the 1700s to import hand-painted wallpapers from China to the United States. Even today, these papers are still completely hand-painted by artisans in China at a studio run by descendants of the same family Charles Gracie worked with in the 1920s. Gracie specializes in custom orders that are designed to fit perfectly within the architecture of a room. Papers can be custom-colored as well as altered to include personalized elements or even designed completely from scratch. Gracie's heritage is such that you can order any design they've ever carried, because they are painted to order. Floral designs have always been the most popular, according to Mike Gracie. "The floral designs give you a feeling of openness and beauty. There's a lot of space between the flowers and the branches, so the background color really comes through," says Gracie. "These papers look beautiful in any size room—you can make a big space grand or make a small space feel more open."

OPPOSITE AND FOLLOWING PAGES: I loved the exquisite hand-painted Gracie wallpaper in my dressing room in our former apartment in New York, which was similar to the wallpaper my grandmother Estée had in her dining room. In our new apartment, my dressing room is swathed in the palest peach-pink silk that's been hand-painted with white and gray monochromatic flowering branches to stunning effect.

The vintage French chandelier in my New York dressing room has
blossom-like clusters of amethyst and clear crystals. Flowers are
also captured in these vintage David Webb brooches fashioned from
pavé diamonds that add a sparkling feminine touch to any outfit.

Brighten the Workday

I almost always have flowers on my desk both in the office and at home. Just a few blooms are such an important antidote to all the time we spend looking at computer screens. Flowers are signs of life that remind me to slow down, to take a moment to daydream, or to think over a problem—a form of visual meditation. Flowers, and fragrance, are at the heart of what I do. They center me, help me regain my focus, or just bring a pause of pleasure and delight to my day-to-day.

OPPOSITE AND FOLLOWING PAGES: Whether it's a desk in your home or at the office, I think it's always a special spot for a small vase of flowers, where you'll see and enjoy them all day. This ebonized Louis XV desk in our Palm Beach living room is an especially formal example, but I also have a shagreen vanity table from AERIN in the bedroom. It could be just a bloom or two in a bud vase or a rich bouquet of peonies, but don't overlook the opportunity to bring beauty to your workday.

"One exquisite flower
in a simple container can
be as magnificent as
a roomful of flowers."

—*Estée Lauder*

OPPOSITE AND FOLLOWING PAGES: True to my grandmother's edict, a small gold
vase with just a few lovely Icelandic poppies brings joy to afternoon tea
or coffee and lets you focus on the beauty of each individual blossom.
Estée taught me that it was worth making the effort to use nice china and
a linen napkin—that anything worth doing is worth doing well.

A bright pop of pink cheers up any workday. And when you have flowers on
your desk such as these ebullient peonies, you can enjoy watching every phase
of their bloom, from tight buds to full-blown blossoms over the course of a week.

Warm and Inviting

Flowers don't always need to be delicate and feminine—they can be bold and strong as well. For a man's desk, study, or bar, I tend to choose deeper colors like purple or chocolate, or neutrals like white and green, rather than more feminine pinks. Added to a mix of handsome shagreen and brass desk accessories, flowers complement an office or study in a sophisticated, elegant way. Plants are also an excellent choice for more masculine spaces. Opt for strong silhouettes, deep colors, or boldly scaled plants, branches and flowers, especially in rooms that are dark or more neutral.

On my husband's desk, small bouquets of hellebores and clematis and touches of gold brighten charcoal-gray shagreen desk accessories.

"There is much more to flowers than just beauty. As a subject, they combine botany and history and architecture— it's almost like creating a well-designed structure. It's half engineering, which I love, and half art, which I also love."

—*Vladimir Kanevsky*
Porcelain artist

I began collecting Vladimir Kanevsky's porcelain flowers after discovering them in Charlotte Moss's store in New York City. My friend, architect and decorator Daniel Romualdez, generously gifted me this extraordinary Vladimir porcelain sculpture of a rose toward the end of its bloom, which I think has a special poignancy.

Private Sanctuary

While I always add a small bouquet of fresh flowers in the powder room when I'm entertaining, I think it's just as lovely to treat yourself to flowers in your own bathroom, where you can enjoy them as you get ready each morning or have a relaxing bath in the evening. Orchids love the humidity, and as long as they get some indirect sunlight, they'll flower for at least a month or two, with very little effort on your part. Plants like ferns also live very happily in a bathroom. A small bouquet of fragrant flowers—gardenias, roses, freesia, sweet peas, lilacs, or hyacinth—will naturally scent the room while bringing fresh life and color to an often monochromatic space. Add a vase in the mix of toiletries and cosmetics on your vanity, a shelf, or windowsill to create a pretty still life. (Placing it beside a mirror will double its impact.) As with your bedside, flowers can have a very uplifting effect when they're the first and last thing you see each day.

Make a guest bath especially inviting with a small bouquet of flowers, like these pink sweet peas, pretty guest towels (I love these feminine rose ones from D. Porthault), and soaps. The floral motif ties into the subtle fern-patterned walls in this powder room. FOLLOWING PAGES: Three charming petite arrangements of peach Icelandic poppies and pink peonies surround the sink beneath a Venetian-glass mirror. A porcelain peony from Italy and AERIN accessories with touches of gold create an elegant vanity.

The Fountain of Youth

One of my grandmother Estée's first innovations came with the introduction of Youth-Dew in 1953, a perfumed bath oil that she intuited women would feel comfortable buying for themselves. Until that time, women traditionally relied on the men in their lives to purchase fragrance for them as a gift. Youth-Dew's spicy floral fragrance quickly caught on, and it was soon introduced as an enduring perfume as well. Its curvaceous, cinched bottle from the 1960s, tied with a bow, is still gracing vanities and dressers today.

In our New York powder room, beneath a gilded Rateau mirror, a gilt vase holds mauve hellebores, miraculous winter flowers that remind us spring will come. FOLLOWING PAGES: In my own bath, the palest pink marble casts a flattering glow, echoed by sweet peas in a silver vase on the vanity and a silver cachepot of pansy orchids by the bathtub. I love the scent and beauty of flowers in the bath.

OPPOSITE: I love that our powder room in Palm Beach has a small vanity area with a console and mirror to touch up your makeup. Beautiful, embroidered fern fabric from Zimmer + Rohde covers the walls with a quiet motif. A small vase of ferns and a pair of antique silvered lamps with rock-crystal flower vines subtly tie into the walls. ABOVE: A delicate porcelain lily-of-the-valley sculpture by Vladimir Kanevsky brings delight year-round.

The Magic of the Holidays

When it comes to the holidays, my mantra is more is more. I entertain more, my family is home, and people are stopping by frequently. I'm caught up in the beauty, festivity, and joy of the season, and I want to express that all throughout my home. Verdant evergreen garlands studded with pine cones are draped across each mantel down to the floor, filling rooms with the wonderful fragrance of the forest. I light scented candles like Megève Rose, with spicy notes of rose, cypress, and balsam fir. If white is often my signature shade of flower the rest of the year, in December it becomes red. I mix rich, vibrant red flowers like roses, peonies, mums, ranunculus, and tulips with berried branches of *Hypericum*, winterberry, and viburnum. When paired with foliage, you have the red and green of traditional holiday celebrations, but touches of deep-purple flowers like hellebores and anemones add depth and sophistication. If you don't have room for a Christmas tree or will be traveling, garlands, wreaths, and luscious red flowers will instantly transform your home for the holidays. I find that the warmth and elegance of gold vases are just the right complement to red. I've collected many over the years and have also designed them for our AERIN line in urnlike shapes that support flowers well for easy arranging. The shimmering gleam of gold together with red and green, gathered on a mantel or used in a centerpiece, says "holiday" to me.

Simple but abundant evergreen garlands studded with pine cones draped across the mantel and the glow of candles and a fire are all it takes to conjure the holiday spirit. FOLLOWING PAGES: Fiery arrangements of red flowers and berries such as dahlias, *Hypericum*, astilbe, dark hellebores, and purple *Astrantia* in gold vases bring brilliance to holiday settings.

The holidays are my favorite time to be in New York City. My recipe for holiday decorating is simple: lush red floral arrangements, gold vases, and evergreen garlands, which bring fragrance and warmth to every room.

ABOVE, OPPOSITE, AND FOLLOWING PAGES: Whether it's just a few peonies, a dazzling array of roses, or a carefully composed arrangement of dahlias, spray roses, peonies, *Hypericum* berries, and ranunculus, with viburnum berries brightening each plate—red, green, and gold are a timeless combination.

Cocktail Hour

Is there any space more seductive than a well-designed bar? From Claridge's in London with its smoky mirrors to the brightly tiled outdoor bar at Cuixmala, the eco resort in Mexico, these inviting spaces beckon us to gather with friends for great conversation. Whether it's a well-outfitted tray on a console table or a bar cart or an alcove in your living or dining room, creating a dedicated space for drinks improves the flow of a party, puts guests at ease, and makes it easy for everyone to serve themselves. When I'm entertaining—indoors or out—I always try to find a space, whether a buffet or a tray table, to set up a small bar. Amidst the ice bucket, glasses, and bottles, I always make room for a small vase of flowers. They immediately draw the eye, adding color and a sense of vitality. Whether I'm using rattan bar accessories outdoors or elegant silver or gold in the city, flowers always layer in a welcoming touch.

My grandparents' former town house in Manhattan has an extraordinary mahogany-paneled bar next to the dining room, which my parents still use for special events and family holidays. It's as well-appointed and sophisticated as any fine restaurant or hotel bar and was always buzzing with activity during the many dinner parties Estée and Joe hosted. Estée loved red roses, in particular, and there would almost always be a sumptuous bouquet of them on the bar.

At the mahogany-paneled bar in my grandparents' New York town house, lavish bouquets of red roses and tall branches set the scene for glamorous entertaining, along with a classic black Norma Kamali gown.

In our new Upper East Side apartment, we were delighted to discover a rather amazing vintage bar off the dining room. It's lined with antiqued mirror and has these wonderful whimsical hand-painted monkeys getting into all kinds of mischief like pouring out bottles, pulling out glassware, and hiding in vases. We preserved these delightful details while updating some of the cabinetry and fixtures. The mirrored backdrop is lined with glass shelves that amplify my collections of silver mint julep cups, crystal decanters, and glassware. I love to collect beautiful spirits bottles and add all the accoutrements, from a large hammered-silver ice bucket to a martini shaker, coasters, trays, bowls for lemons and limes, linen cocktail napkins, and silver vases for flowers. But you certainly don't need a dedicated bar to serve cocktails cordially. Even when you're simply serving drinks on a tray, adding a small nosegay in a bud vase will take your hospitality to the next level.

All it takes to create a bar on any table, buffet, or surface is a tray, glassware, cocktail napkins, and some nibbles. I always like to add a small vase of flowers to bring color and life to the setting and make it even more inviting.

Our new apartment has a wonderful mirror-lined bar in an alcove off the dining room. If you look closely, you can see one of the whimsical monkeys (at left) who are making mischief with the glassware. I lined the glass shelves with silver mercury glass cups, glassware, decanters, handsome liquor bottles, and bar accoutrements. A silver vase of purple hyacinth adds a bright spot of color.

Gleaming gold accessories—from an
ice bucket to gold-rimmed glassware—
instantly elevate a bar, while a
faceted gold vase holds an array of
deep-red peonies, delicate purple
columbine, and wispy stems of penny-
cress, all worthy of a Dutch still life.

Wherever I am, I like to adapt my entertaining style and bar setup accordingly. At the beach, that usually means relying on natural, textural materials like rattan, wicker, and raffia. In our pool house in Palm Beach, a rattan table organizes glassware and accessories like a wicker-wrapped ice bucket and wine cooler and a whimsical silver pineapple ice bucket. A small bowl of kumquats and a maidenhair fern in a woven wicker basket introduce vibrant color that echoes the tropical wallpaper. I'll use shells as weights to keep cocktail napkins from blowing in the breeze and add colorful glassware and napkins. In the mountains come fall and winter, I often choose rustic wooden trays and bowls, horn-handled bar tools, tortoiseshell glassware, and a vase of berries and evergreens.

I think a bar can be a great place to have fun and introduce colorful artisanal glassware and coasters, and playful shapes in vases and decanters. On a rustic wood-and-cane chest in Panama, I set up a bar with bright, flowered Murano glassware, bamboo lanterns and wicker-wrapped bottles, simple palm fronds clipped from the yard and placed in pottery vases, including a charming bird-shaped pitcher, and a few coconuts from outside. A shelf above it offers a home for sapphire-hued bubble glassware. Even in this rustic setting, a bar offers a grace note of hospitality and enjoyment.

For a more tropical take on a bar, I outfitted a set of rattan shelves in our Florida pool house with natural wicker accessories, a whimsical silver pineapple ice bucket, a maidenhair fern in a basket, and a bowl of bright kumquats to pick up on the island flora depicted in the wallpaper. FOLLOWING PAGES: In Panama, candles in woven rattan hurricanes cast a warm glow, while Murano glassware and vases with palm fronds add vibrant color. I like to draw on whatever's at hand—shells, coconuts, limes—to add local flavor.

Tropical Paradise

Two decades ago, my husband, Eric, started traveling with friends down to Panama to surf and fish in a very remote area on the Pacific coast. Eventually he started taking our sons there for "boys' trips," roughing it in rustic camps. This far-flung Eden became a passion of Eric's. He and a couple close friends purchased a barren piece of property and embarked on a reforestation and environmental conservation project. I'm proud that his efforts over time have reintroduced more than seventy-five species of trees and a wealth of flora and fauna—birds, monkeys, crocodiles, even pumas—to what is now an ecological preserve. A few years ago, he began working with architects Ivan and Kristin Morales on a house that he wanted to feel like a treehouse—truly indoor-outdoor and very open, using all-natural materials to create teak-and-bamboo pavilions with thatched roofs. The pavilions are connected by gardens and outdoor walkways and elevated for natural cross-ventilation and to take in the views, so I always feel at one with nature when I am there. Once the forest was mature, the architects were able to harvest wood from the property to build much of the furniture with the help of local craftspeople. It's a truly magical spot, like an enchanted island. You just feel so far, far away from everything—because you actually are. The nearest town is a very long, bumpy, unpaved road away.

At our house in Panama, everything is natural and easy. I simply gather what's outside, like these large palm fronds, to make a simple but dramatic arrangement in a large-scale white ceramic vase with whimsical parrots. Life here is a barefoot affair, but I still enjoy dresses with a tropical flair, such as this one by Johanna Ortiz.

ABOVE, OPPOSITE, AND PREVIOUS PAGES: A table set with the all-natural textures of wicker, rattan, bamboo, and raffia draws on the organic plant material found in this area and melds easily with AERIN x Casa Lopez tableware. Orchids and many other beautiful flowers grow naturally here, including these orange cymbidium and epidendrum orchids.

When we're in Panama, it's all about relying on the uncomplicated beauty of the native vegetation, from palm fronds to tropical orchids. There are no florists—I simply walk around the property clipping flowers and greenery to create very relaxed, natural arrangements. Raffia, wicker, and bamboo vases and table settings blend in easily; some artisan-crafted ceramic vases add a little color and variety. The bright oranges, yellows, and pinks of freesia and orchids stand out brilliantly against the woods and textured materials. The beauty of a tropical climate, whether Panama or Florida, is that there are always flowers in season and as close as the backyard. In Palm Beach, there's vibrant fuchsia bougainvillea spilling over stucco walls everywhere, along with the heady fragrance of jasmine and gardenia. It is a flower-lover's dream and a gift to experience such beauty at every turn. We almost always eat outdoors, where we're surrounded by nature, and flowers on the table are just an extension of the flowers and foliage all around us. Putting together bouquets is effortless. I like to create multiple small arrangements that can be easily mixed with votive candles or hurricanes, and that give me the flexibility to decorate a long rectangular table or a round one with ease. Flowers are not a special-occasion luxury in these warm-weather climates, they surround us every day in abundance.

Brighten poolside or patio drinks with flowers, such as this tiny bouquet of orchids in a glass vase with a raffia sleeve. Citrus slices and sprigs of mint provide a refreshing garnish for frozen cocktails or smoothies.

"I've always been fascinated by the language of femininity as well as the language of flowers. Their complexity and their beauty are something I draw inspiration from again and again."

—*Erdem Moralioglu*
Creative Director and Founder, ERDEM

The scale of the palms and plants in Florida is quite dramatic, and on this curved walkway to our front gates carved from weathered Cuban coral, they immerse us in greenery year-round. I love wearing ERDEM's brilliant floral patterns and feminine designs in this tropical setting.

The Respite of Green

There is something inherently refreshing and calming about greenery. In fact, plants have been shown to induce relaxation and even lower stress hormones. A verdant touch that lasts longer than flowers, greenery invites nature indoors and, in the case of plants and trees, can thrive for years with proper care. I'm particularly partial to ferns. Their lacy fronds bring a delicate yet luxuriant counterpoint to any room—perfect in a kitchen, sunporch, bedroom, or study.

Potted trees and topiaries take greenery a step further, bringing elegant height and a focal point to a room. I love the symmetry of a pair of trees flanking a window. Fruit or flowering trees like calamondin oranges, Meyer lemons, hibiscus, or gardenia standards add appealing splashes of color and scent in season. But the silvery green of olive trees or the deep emerald of a palm are equally compelling year-round. The planter you choose is just as important a decorative element, whether it's an elegant chinoiserie jardiniere or a simple basket.

Think of plants and trees as architectural elements in a room, while flowers are vibrant accessories that steal the show for a little while.

The marble checkerboard entry to our Palm Beach house looks very similar to my grandparents' foyer. A simple white vase filled with graceful palm fronds clipped from outside is all it takes to make a grand entrance. FOLLOWING PAGES: I find arrangements filled with greenery especially serene, and they also last longer. I love these sculptural Corvo Vases from AERIN that have a modern, abstract form and organic texture inspired by coral and shells.

Holding Beauty

I find it very relaxing and fulfilling to arrange flowers. No two arrangements will ever look exactly alike—each has its own special beauty. Pairing flowers with the right vase is an art in itself: you want a vase that's the right shape and size to bring out the best in the flowers, and vice versa. Will you be gathering soft, pliable tulips that could use some support? Stately stems of iris requiring a tall vase? A delicate nosegay of lily of the valley that needs a small vase with a narrow neck? Often what's most relevant to arranging flowers is the size of the neck, or opening, of the vase. Urn or trumpet shapes that curve inward help support and position flowers, while cylindrical columns can be ideal for tall stems and branches. A low bowl or a vase with a wide mouth will likely need a flower frog or ball of chicken wire to help anchor the flower stems and provide a structure to hold them in place.

There is an abundant array of vases to choose from, but it helps to have a foundational wardrobe of containers in classic shapes—urns, short and tall cylinders, bowls, mint julep cups, perhaps a square cube. And, of course, containers that are not traditional vases work just as well, like pitchers, bottles, glasses, or baskets with liners. I have some beautiful vintage, antique, and artisanal vases I've collected over the years that go beyond basic forms to elevate a whole arrangement.

A woven basket can be a wonderful cachepot for a plant, such as this maidenhair fern, or a vase, as long as it has a glass, ceramic, or plastic liner that is watertight. I like to collect silver vases with varied decoration, such as these with heart and bucket-like detailing. They're lovely to mix and match. FOLLOWING PAGES: This dramatic, Deco-style French vase by Georges Jouve from the 1940s has two openings, which makes for an especially exuberant arrangement, such as these boughs of viburnum. Rippled and seeded glass adds interest to clear vases holding loose arrangements of clematis.

The material of the vase comes into play as well: Simple clear glass or crystal works with everything (though keep in mind that the stems will be visible). White ceramic, silver, or gold are always classic. Or choose something entirely different, like wood or metal. Though I often opt for solid colors, vases with beautiful patterns, like a blue-and-white chinoiserie urn, can be quite special. While most colors and materials can work with a wide range of flowers, there's an artistry to pairing flowers with just the right vase that enhances both. You can enjoy experimenting with different options while you get a feel for what works best.

There are some general rules of thumb that might help as a starting point: For a dinner table centerpiece, keep arrangements low (generally, under twelve inches) so that guests can see and converse over the flowers. For low vases, the height of the flowers is ideally about one and a half times the height of the container, and up to two times the width, but these are by no means hard-and-fast rules. For tall vases, flowers that are about two and a half times the height of your container create a pleasing proportion.

Be sure to condition your flowers as soon as you bring them home by cutting their stems at an angle, removing all foliage that will be below the waterline, and placing them in cool water, ideally mixed with a vitamin powder like the packets you get from your florist. Add a couple of drops of bleach to prevent the growth of bacteria and change the water every couple of days. Treat flowers well, and they'll reward you by lasting longer.

The concave shape of this textured silver vase helps to anchor the flowers. The strong form also helps balance the bold peppermint-striped tulips. FOLLOWING PAGES: The pleasingly curved shapes of these ceramic and Murano glass vases from AERIN have narrowed necks to support flowers and hold them in place.

Bringing Nature Indoors

Flowering branches make a dramatic statement. I love their airy, sculptural grace—the glorious beauty of a tree in early spring transported inside. You can force flowering branches like quince, apple, cherry, or magnolia toward the end of winter to coax along spring and experience their joy on the gray days of March. Their branches will unfurl over a period of days and weeks, bringing ever-changing wonder. Because of their commanding height, place them in a spot where they can take center stage, whether it's in a foyer or on a console table in the living room, on a kitchen island, or as punctuation at the end of a hallway. Nestle them in a tall, sturdy vase or urn so they are rooted securely, then add water regularly and enjoy their beauty.

In the entry to our New York apartment, a large plaster Giacometti vase from the 1930s is a sculptural home for large branches, such as these camellia boughs. I bought the eighteenth-century Beauvais tapestry many years ago in Paris with my parents, and it has created a dramatic backdrop everywhere I've lived. FOLLOWING PAGES: A shapely Alvar Aalto vase helps support vibrant red peonies in the library. Branches of quince form a dramatic arrangement on a small leaf-shaped table.

It brings hopes of spring to watch tiny buds unfurl into blossoms when you force flowering branches, such as these quince, in late winter. Parrot tulips, cut short and clustered in a low, dimpled glass vase, are equally beautiful to watch open.

238

Natural Textures

Because they are made from plant materials themselves, I find that raffia, straw, wicker, and rattan vases, baskets, and containers all work particularly well with flowers. They provide a natural backdrop for any type of flower, particularly in summer, and are well-suited to outdoor and more informal settings. Woven baskets can't hold water but can be fitted with watertight glass, metal, or plastic containers. Whether on a summer table, outdoor patio, or indoor sunroom, these planters and vases provide airy texture that works effortlessly with plants and blossoms, and are a worthy addition to your repertoire of containers.

I find myself using these pretty woven raffia sleeves on glass cylinder vases all the time in summer, when their natural ease is a perfect match for simple garden blossoms. The airy pattern looks equally pretty holding a candle.

"My grandmother planted wonderfully fragrant lilac bushes surrounding her East Hampton house that burst into bloom each May. These lilacs continue to thrive and inspired one of my favorite AERIN fragrances, Lilac Path. Nothing else quite equals the heady scent that fills my home for the treasured weeks that lilacs bloom."

—*Aerin Lauder*

OPPOSITE AND FOLLOWING PAGES: Lilacs come in such a pretty range of hues, from white to pale lavender to deep purple, and they mix beautifully with the fresh spring green of viburnum. Their effusive blossoms look especially pretty in woven wicker baskets and cachepots.

"Every flower is my favorite. Every flower has its own beauty."

—Frances Palmer
Ceramicist and avid gardener

One of my favorite handcrafted Frances Palmer vases is in my kitchen, here holding cherry blossoms. The classic form balanced with handmade details such as scored lines and delicate rows of beading give it artistry and charm.

In a special collection for AERIN, Frances Palmer handcrafted these shapely
vases in white earthenware clay coated in a pale lavender slip and then a clear
glaze for a luminous hint of color. It picks up on the soft purple hues of the clematis
beautifully. Tiny daisies offer a charming complement to the larger blossoms.

PREVIOUS PAGES: This charming bird-shaped Anka Vase, inspired by a midcentury vase, whimsically holds flowers in its head.
RIGHT: The ocean-blue glaze of these AERIN vases beautifully complements loose, natural arrangements of wildflowers and garden blossoms like bright-pink cosmos, Queen Anne's lace, daisies, and loosestrife.

Inspiration at Work

It may not seem so unexpected now, but in the business world of the 1960s, my grandmother Estée's office was quite unusual in its unabashed femininity and glamour. Perched on the fortieth floor of the General Motors building, her spacious suite, decorated with hand-painted floral Gracie wallpaper, plush sofas, wall-to-wall carpet, and floor-length curtains resembled an elegant home more than a corporate office. Estée taught me that since we spend so much time at the office, it should be as comfortable and lovely as possible—with fresh flowers, a pretty water carafe and glasses, china plates, and teacups. One of her mantras was that "everything can be beautiful if you take the time."

Estée's voice was in my mind when I had the opportunity to design our offices for the AERIN brand. The offices are in the beautiful Art Deco Fuller Building on Madison Avenue and Fifty-Seventh Street, in the heart of Manhattan. As the showcase for our beauty and home brand but also our day-to-day workspace, I want it not only to be beautiful but also to feel welcoming and to inspire creativity. The interior design by Jacques Grange laid the foundation for this exquisite space, with luxuriously comfortable sofas,

The Madison Avenue offices of the AERIN brand are decorated like an elegant but welcoming home, always with plants and fresh flowers, such as these brilliant Icelandic poppies. FOLLOWING PAGES: In the creative studio, desks are clustered together and flowers and personal touches such as raffia trays and Murano pitchers brighten our workspace. Deep-pink hyacinths and sunny-yellow ranunculus delight and inspire us.

Product samples and inspiration, including vases, trays, and frames, line a wall of file cabinets in the design studio. Beautifully handcrafted paper flowers, including a white fritillaria and red tulips by Livia Cetti of The Green Vase in Brooklyn, and on the wall, pressed flower artwork by Tricia Paoluccio of Modern Pressed Flower, help ideas take root.

sparkling lighting, and elegant vitrines, but fresh flowers throughout the office undoubtedly make it feel vibrant, inviting, and inspiring. In addition to orchids and plants in each area, we have fresh flower arrangements designed by the talented Raúl Àvila delivered weekly. I consider this an essential luxury in a business such as fragrance, beauty, and design, where flowers play such an integral role. For that reason, there are flowers—as well as floral art—not only in the reception area but also on the desks and worktables of our creative studio. Pretty straw trays used as inboxes, vases we've designed or are working on, Murano glasses and water pitchers all bring beauty to everyone's desks and workdays. Having a colorful bouquet of flowers to ponder and breathe in while dreaming up new ideas can't help but inspire our creativity and add a pause of pleasure to a busy day. Flowers are at the heart of what we do, but you certainly don't need to be in the beauty business to experience the benefits of making the place where you work as warm and welcoming as possible.

OPPOSITE AND FOLLOWING PAGES: Every day is a beautiful collage of ideas, inspiration, research, and work in progress, from fragrance samples to photo shoot mood boards. A pretty white ceramic cachepot with a rose handle is an idea for a candle vessel, while white porcelain dahlias are existing products. Vintage botanical engravings and a brilliant bouquet might help inspire packaging or perfume ideas.

"I grew up in Colombia, surrounded by beauty in nature, but it's not like we had flowers in our home. When I moved here, I started working for Robert Isabell, and my passion for flowers grew. I never imagined that I could be where I am now, surrounded by beauty every day."

— *Raúl Àvila*
New York City floral designer
and event planner

Ranunculus and poppies in brilliant yellows, pinks, and oranges offer a rejuvenating reminder of spring in the midst of winter.

Estée always believed in taking the time to do things beautifully,
even at work—such as a proper afternoon tea with gold-rimmed china
and elegant gold petit fours from Bon Vivant. Vibrant pink hyacinths
in a gold vase amplify the sofa's feminine hue.

Resources

FLORAL DESIGN

New York
Raúl Àvila
Event planning and floral design
Raúl is my go-to floral designer
for our offices, my home, and many
special events. His creativity and
talent, whether he's designing
the Met Gala or top fashion shows,
is unparalleled.
raulavilainc.com

Zezé
I love Zezé's colorful, exuberant,
and always optimistic bouquets
to send to friends or to decorate
my tables.
938 First Avenue
New York, New York 10022
212-753-7767

The Bridgehampton Florist
Michael Grim at Bridgehampton
Florist is my source for naturalistic
arrangements with fresh-from-
the-garden beauty.
thebridgehamptonflorist.com

Florida
Tom Mathieu
Tom Mathieu does it all—from orchids and
topiaries to lush flower arrangements.
tommathieu.com

England
Willow Crossley
Based in the Cotswolds, Willow Crossley
creates loose, organic bouquets of garden
blossoms and wildflowers feel like they've
been plucked straight from nature.
willowcrossley.com

Paris
Castor-Fleuriste
In Paris, Louis-Géraud Castor draws on
a background in art to create sculptural,
sophisticated arrangements and events
for top fashion houses and individual
clients alike.
By Appointment Only
castor-fleuriste.com

Eric Chauvin
Chauvin Paris
This floral genius whose fantastical
creations grace many fashion shows
also focuses on natural, pesticide-free
flower growing.
chauvinparis.com

ARTISTS AND ARTISANS

Clare Potter
Finely crafted bouquets of porcelain
flowers are painstakingly handmade by
Clare with layers of color washes, rather
than glazes, for a highly realistic yet
unquestionably artistic feel.
clarepotter.com

Frances Palmer
A brilliant ceramicist, Frances studies
ancient forms then crafts whimsical
modern vases that are all her own.
francespalmerpottery.com

The Green Vase
Artist Livia Cetti crafts lifelike flowering
plants entirely from paper and has
also written two how-to books on
paper-flower crafting.
thegreenvase.com

Modern Pressed Flower
Tricia Paoluccio is an artist known for her
distinctive botanical collages and
pressed-flower art. She also teaches
online and in-person classes in flower-
pressing techniques.
modernpressedflower.com

Tommy Mitchell
Tommy practices the centuries-old art of
tole—enameled metalwork—to create
beautiful, lifelike flowering plants.
tommymitchellcompany.com

Vladimir Kanevsky
An extraordinarily gifted artist, Vladimir
hand sculpts delicate flowering bouquets
and plants from porcelain that are
coveted by collectors worldwide.
For inquiries: 201-592-1176
vladimirkanevsky.com

VASES AND TABLEWARE

AERIN
Reflecting my passion for flowers, we've
designed and curated a beautiful array of
vases for every size and style of bouquet,
along with captivating tableware
collections to help you entertain in style.
aerin.com

Bergdorf Goodman
The seventh floor of this landmark New
York City store features an expertly
curated collection of elegant vases,
tabletop, and dining accessories.
bergdorfgoodman.com

Carolina Irving & Daughters
Textile designer Carolina Irving and her
daughters, Olympia and Ariadne, offer
beautiful collections of handcrafted and
hand-painted pottery for the table, along
with vases, block-printed tablecloths,
and accessories.
ci-daughters.com

Christopher Spitzmiller
Christopher is best-known for his sculptural,
gourd-like lamps, but he also designs
beautiful vases, tableware, and more.
christopherspitzmiller.com

James Robinson
This storied Park Avenue store offers an elegant curation of antique and new silver, porcelain, glass, and ceramics.
jrobinson.com

La Tuile à Loup
Owner Eric Goujou travels all over France to find the finest artisanal pottery, including vases and exquisite tableware.
latuilealoup.com

March
My favorite home store in San Francisco offers a distinguished modern edit of decor, furniture, fine art, and tabletop accessories.
marchsf.com

Museum of Modern Art Design Store
From Alvar Aalto's wavy glass vase to the defining icons of the past century, MoMA offers the best of modern design for home and tabletop.
store.moma.org

Neue Galerie
The design shop of this museum focusing on Austrian and German art offers objets based on designs from Biedermeier to the Bauhaus as well as renowned contemporary designers.
shop.neuegalerie.org

Scully & Scully
This is a Park Avenue institution for timeless, elegant pieces from silver and china to crystal and flatware.
scullyandscully.com

Talmaris
This is the place to go in Paris for remarkable table settings filled with color, creativity, and artistry.
By appointment only
+33 1 42 88 20 20
Instagram: @talmaris.paris

TABLE & BED LINENS, FABRICS AND WALLPAPER

AERIN Fabrics for Lee Jofa (to the trade)
kravet.com

Bennison Fabrics
bennisonfabrics.com

Carolina Irving
carolinairvingtextiles.com

Colefax & Fowler
www.colefax.com

Cowtan & Tout
cowtan.com

D. Porthault
The finest quality bed and table linens in a garden of floral patterns and palettes.
dporthaultparis.com

Gracie Wallpaper
A family-run business for over a century, Gracie offers exquisite hand-painted wallpapers and custom murals that can transform any room into a garden or landscape.
graciestudio.com

Leontine Linens
One of the best sources in the country for custom-monogrammed table and bed linens.
leontinelinens.com

Lisa Fine Textiles
lisafinetextiles.com

Zimmer + Rohde
zimmer-rohde.com

FOODS

Bon Vivant New York
Maya Hormis and her team create charming petit fours that feature intricate flowers and gilding. They are based in Jersey City but deliver to Manhattan and ship nationwide.
bonvivantnewyork.com

Made in Heaven Cakes
Pastry chef Victoria Zagami runs the Brooklyn cake business her parents started, creating their signature Flower Pot cakes as well as custom wedding and celebration cakes featuring exquisite sugar flowers.
madeinheavencakes.com

Sant Ambroeus
My favorite coffee and dessert bar in New York, as well as in Palm Beach and Aspen.
Multiple locations in the US and Europe
santambroeus.com

FASHION & JEWELRY

Fred Leighton
fredleighton.com

Belperron
belperron.com

Verdura
verdura.com

Erdem (cover dress)
erdem.com

Giambattista Valli pg 16, 37
giambattistavalli.com

INVITATIONS/STATIONERY

Smythson
smythson.com

Acknowledgments

My deepest gratitude to all the incredibly talented people who helped create this book:

First and foremost, the florists I love to collaborate with and always look to for inspiration and beauty: Raúl Àvila, Zezé Calvo, Michael Grim, and Tom Mathieu, who I've known and worked with for many years, as well as newer discoveries such as Willow Crossley, Louis-Géraud Castor, and Eric Chauvin.

Thank you to the photographers Thomas Loof, Mark Lund, and Mason Lane for the beautiful images that brought this book to life, and for your constant optimism and support on set.

A special thank-you to Burcu Cizmecioglu, my creative partner at AERIN for more than ten years, who makes everything look perfect and never fails to find new ways to approach each design.

My gratitude to Doug Turshen and Steve Turner for their creative vision and patience in turning photographs and ideas into the captivating book you hold in your hands.

Thank you to the team at Rizzoli, especially my publisher Charles Miers and editor Ellen Nidy, for believing in and supporting my vision for a book on flowers.

To my hair and makeup artist Alexa Rodulfo, thank you for always making me look and feel my best.

Thank you to my boys for their belief in me—I know deep down they appreciate the beauty of the flowers I am forever bringing into our homes.

And finally, thank you to my husband, Eric, my constant supporter and motivator for more than three decades. He encouraged me to start AERIN and follow my dreams. After so many years, he knows that flowers are the key to my heart. No matter how big or small the bouquet, they always make me smile.

PHOTOGRAPHY CREDITS:

Camilla Akrans / AUGUST: 8, 36-37

Stanley B. Burns, MD and The Burns Archive: 12

Anita Calero / Supervision: 212

Gabor Jurina: 130-131, 201, 255

Nick Krasznai: 17

Elizabeth Kuhner, Lauder Family Collection: page 4

Francesca Lagnese / OTTO: 99, 101

Mason Lane: 104, 271

Mark Lund: 2, 5, 11, 30, 31, 32, 35, 39, 41, 42-43, 44, 48-49, 50, 51, 55, 56-57, 59, 60, 61, 64, 65, 66, 67, 88, 89, 100, 102-103, 106-107, 108-109, 110, 114-115, 116, 117, 118, 119, 120, 122-123, 124, 125, 129, 132-133, 162, 163, 166-167, 168, 171, 172, 178-179, 188-189, 192, 193, 196, 197, 198-199, 202, 206-207, 210-211, 214-215, 216, 217, 218, 224, 225, 229, 231, 232, 233, 237, 238-239, 241, 243-245, 246, 248, 249, 250, 251, 252-253, 256-257, 258-259, 260, 262-263, 265, 266, 267

Thomas Loof @ Art Department NY: 6, 19, 20, 21, 23, 24, 33, 46, 79, 80-81, 83, 84, 85, 86, 91, 92-93, 94, 95, 97, 112, 126, 137, 140, 146, 147, 149, 150, 151, 154, 157, 160, 161, 164, 170, 175, 176, 180, 182, 183, 185, 187, 190, 191, 204, 205, 208, 221, 227, 228, 235, 236

Fred J. Maroon: 9, 14

Norman Parkinson / Iconic Images: 12

John Peden: 12

Ben Pogue: 69, 71

Genevieve Stevenson: 63

© Simon Upton @simonuptonphotos.com: 25, 26-27, 29, 73, 74-75, 76-77, 134-135, 141, 142, 144, 153, 155, 159, 184, 194-195, 222

First published in the
United States of America in 2025 by
Rizzoli International Publications, Inc.
49 West 27th Street
New York, NY 10001
www.rizzoliusa.com

Copyright © Aerin Lauder
Texts: Jill Simpson

Publisher: Charles Miers
Editor: Ellen Nidy
Design: Doug Turshen with Steve Turner
Production Manager: Colin Hough Trapp
Managing Editor: Lynn Scrabis

ISBN: 978-0-8478-4384-8
Library of Congress Control Number: 2025193406

Printed in Italy
2025 2026 2027 2028 / 10 9 8 7 6 5 4 3 2 1

Visit us online:
Instagram.com/RizzoliBooks
Facebook.com/RizzoliNewYork
X: @Rizzoli_Books
Youtube.com/user/RizzoliNY